Understanding Financial Statement Analysis

for Accountants, Business Owners, Investors, and Stakeholders

Calvin K. Lee, MBA, CPA, CA, CPA (Illinois)

Table of Contents

Table of Contents

1. What you'll get out of this book

2. Balance Sheet - things to watch for

3. Parts of the balance sheet

4. Is lots of cash always a good thing? Not always.

5. Accounts receivable and sales are going up. Great? Maybe not.

6. Inventory - beware of obsolescence

7. Current assets - your first line of defense in business liquidity

8. Current ratio: can this company survive 1 year?

9. Long-term assets - needed to generate future income

10. Property, plant and equipment (PP&E) - watch how they depreciate

11. Intangible assets - essential for some businesses

12. Goodwill - test for impairment

13. Total assets - read the notes and make sure they are all there

14. Return on Assets - did the company make money?

15. Asset turnover ratio - how much revenue did the company make?

16. Current liabilities - pay or face consequences

17. Accounts payable - keep your cash. Delaying payment is good

18. Income taxes payable - do this legally to avoid going to jail

19. Customers' deposits / deferred revenue - not your money...yet!

20. Debts - are they bad or good? It depends

21. Short-term loans - necessary at crucial times

22. Long-term liabilities - a way to fund the business

23. Debt-to-equity ratio - screw this up at your own risk

24. Shareholder's equity - who owns the company?

25. Return on equity - getting your investment money's worth

26. Income statement

27. Revenue - first thing most people look at

28. Cost of sales - let's keep this low

29. Gross margin / gross profit - did we make a profit?

30. Cash flows - cash is king

Final thoughts

Bonus video on balance sheet concepts

About the Author

Note to the reader

Contact the author

Other books by Calvin K. Lee

FREE book sample from

"How to Increase Confidence and Succeed in Meeting People: Business Networking the Easy Way...Meet New People Now!"

FREE book sample from

"Living an Extraordinary and Amazingly Purposeful Life: 9 Principles to a Better Life"

FREE book sample from

Words of Wisdom, Encouragement, and Inspiration

Calvin K. Lee, MBA, CPA

WORDS OF WISDOM, ENCOURAGEMENT, AND INSPIRATION (BOOK #3)

Bring Happiness into Your Life

FREE book sample from

How to Work Smarter, Not Harder: Success in the Workplace

FREE book sample from

A Collection of Short Stories

FREE book sample from

Bookkeeping and Accounting Step-by-step Basics for Small & Medium sized Businesses and Home Businesses: Over 20 Examples of Common Accounting Transactions!

1. What you'll get out of this book

After reading this book you should have a good understanding of financial statements and reports.

Accounting is the basic language of business. Whether you are an accountant/bookkeeper, a business owner, or an investor, you look at financial statements and reports to determine how well a company is performing.

As a CPA, I look at financial statements every day. I also prepare financial statements for clients. I will share with you in simple terms how to understand and make use of financial statements to achieve your goals.

Where do you start?

Financial statements have several components, including the balance sheet, income statement, cash flow statement, statement of equity, and notes to financial statements.

In my job as a public accountant/auditor I've worked with many different companies. On many days I work with new clients. I have to familiarize myself with the company before doing my audit work.

I start by looking at the notes to the financial statements, usually attached at the end of the financial statements. The notes generally give a good overview of what the company does and introduces the many features in the balance sheet and income statement.

If you're an accountant or bookkeeper who's looking to not only understand financial statements, but also understand the bookkeeping/accounting principles, I suggest you read this book and also my book *"Bookkeeping and Accounting Step-by-step Basics for Small & Medium Sized Businesses and Home Businesses: Over 20 Examples of Common Accounting Transactions!"* (click here to get a copy in Amazon). In that book I show you the basics of how to do bookkeeping.

Bonus video on balance sheet to further explain concepts at the end of this book! Click here to go to end of book now. There will be a link back here.

2. Balance Sheet - things to watch for

The balance sheet is a historical statement. It is a snapshot at a particular time, usually the year-end of the company.

The balance sheet is usually prepared in the time right after the year-end, usually due for filing with the government 2 or 3 months after the year-end.

Example.
Let's say a company has a year-end of December 31. If you are an investor you are entitled to a copy of the financial statements. Let's say you're an investor looking to invest in a company. You get the financial statements in March of the next year.

You have to remember that the financial statements show the financial performance of a company as at December 31. What has happened in the few months after is not reflected on the financial statements.

If there was a lawsuit that happened subsequent to the date of the financial statements, it would not show on the balance sheet. If the company was sold subsequent to the financial statements date, it would not show on the balance sheet. If new technology was introduced subsequent to the financial statements date, it would not show on the balance sheet.

How to account for these subsequent events?

There are several ways. On the notes to the financial statements, there is a section where management may disclose some foreseeable subsequent events. Another way is to try to get interim financial statements for the new fiscal year subsequent to the year-end financial statements.

URL letter: w

3. Parts of the balance sheet

The balance sheet is generally divided into three main parts. They are:
- Assets
- Liabilities
- Equity

Assets represent the tangible and intangible assets of a company. Tangible assets are things like cash and inventory. Intangible assets include things like goodwill, which is formed when a company purchases another company at a price higher than the net assets of the company being acquired.

Why would a company pay a price higher than the net assets?

It's because the company being acquired has a brand or existing customer list that is worth something and valuable to the company that is acquiring, but these items are not listed on the balance sheet of the company being acquired.

URL letter: a

4. Is lots of cash always a good thing? Not always.

The first asset that is listed is usually cash. Many users of the financial statements, such as accountants/bookkeepers, business owners, investors, creditors, and other stakeholders, look at the amount of cash on hand.

A large cash balance is always good, right?

Wrong. Having a lot of cash on the balance sheet may indicate poor management. Let me explain.

Example.
Cash is sometimes listed as "cash and cash equivalents", meaning any short term liquid investments like certificate of deposits of 30 days are included as "cash". Idle cash doesn't help the company grow its asset base. Perhaps it is better if management puts excess idle cash into investments. I've seen this with some companies. They have lots of cash just sitting there when they should invest it in investments or do something else to make use of their excess cash.

Conclusion:
Unless there is a good reason for the cash balance to be large, such as expecting to pay a large bill or make a purchase, a large cash balance could indicate poor management.

URL letter: t

5. Accounts receivable and sales are going up. Great? Maybe not.

A business usually receives payment from customers in several different forms, including cash or on credit, or a combination of the two.

Accounts receivable is a customer promising to pay in the future in exchange for goods or services now. When a business or company starts up, initially it may grant lenient credit policies to attract more customers.

When customers with lower credit rating are allowed to purchase goods or services on credit, there will usually be more sales. The sales on the income statement increases, and so does accounts receivable. Everything is fine, and business is booming, right?

Maybe.

Example.
A large accounts receivable is useless to a company if they cannot collect cash from customers who promise to pay later. Remember cash is king. If a company doesn't receive cash from its customers, it doesn't matter how many millions of dollars of sales it is generating.

A company must still pay Its bills and creditors regardless whether it is collecting cash from its customers or not. Some companies in an attempt to grow sales have done exactly what was described above. But when the company's cash reserves run out, creditors will call loans, and the company may need to fold even though it is generating a lot of sales.

Conclusion:
To put it simply, a large accounts receivable can be a good thing, or it can be a warning sign.

As long as a company can keep collecting cash from its customers listed on the accounts receivable, then it is not in immediate danger. If customers are taking more than 90 days to pay, then the company may have some collection issues.

URL letter: c

6. Inventory - beware of obsolescence

So far we've discussed how a large cash account or a large accounts receivable account can indicate issues with a company.

How about inventory?

This question depends on what kind of inventory the company is selling. If the company is in the high-tech sector and the technology changes rapidly, having a large inventory can be a huge problem because it can become obsolete.

Example.
If a computer company has a lot of inventory of computers that uses a certain type of processing chip, and suddenly a new computer chip technology is introduced making that type of processing chip obsolete, then that inventory can suddenly drop in value.

Generally accepted accounting principles require companies to write down the value of inventory to the lower of its fair market value or book value. Market value is what you can sell the inventory for, and book value is the cost at which you obtained the inventory.

Example.
You purchase 100 computer chips on October 1 for $5 each. You record the following:

Dr. Inventory   500
      Cr. Cash   500
To record purchase of inventory

You have an inventory balance of $500. However, as at December 31 the year-end, the computer chips drop in value and are only worth $300.

The company then must write-down the inventory by $200.

Dr. Loss on write-down on inventory   200
      Cr. Inventory   200
To write-down inventory to fair market value

The inventory balance at the end of the year, December 31, is $300.

Conclusion:
As you can see in the above example, having a large inventory of inventory that is prone to being obsolete due to change in technology or customer preference can be an issue.

URL letter: h

7. Current assets - your first line of defense in business liquidity

In the above sections I've discussed:
- Cash
- Accounts receivable
- Inventory

These are called *current assets.* Current assets are distinguished from long-term assets, such as equipment, in that they are more liquid, meaning they can be converted to cash within one year.

Remember:
Current assets are assets that are liquid, and can be converted into cash within one year. They are distinguished from long-term assets, which typically lasts more than one year.

Current assets are very important to the survival of a business. If a business does not have enough current assets to pay off its current liabilities, then there can be some liquidity issues. This means a company may not be able to pay its short-term debts and has a higher risk of going bankrupt or default.

URL letter: see next chapter!

8. Current ratio: can this company survive 1 year?

The current ratio is a quick tool to determine whether a company can survive one year.

The current ratio is comprised of two components:
- Current assets
- Current liabilities

I have discussed current assets above, and will discuss current liabilities in a later section. You know that current assets are assets that can be turned into cash within one year. Similarly, current liabilities are liabilities that are due within one year.

Example.
Current liabilities include:
- Accounts payable
- Income taxes payable
- Customer deposits

These are examples of liabilities that the company is obligated to pay within the next year. There can be legal and other consequences such as bad creditor relationship or bad vendor relationships for not paying these current liabilities on time.

The current ratio takes current assets and divides the total by current liabilities.

Remember:
Current ratio = current assets / current liabilities

As a general rule of thumb, if current assets = current liabilities, then the current ratio will equal 1.

Example.
A company has $1,000 of current assets and $1,000 of current liabilities. This means the company has just enough current assets to cover all of its

current liabilities that will become due within the next year. The current ratio is 1.

Example.
If the company has twice as much current assets than current liabilities, then the current ratio will be 2:1. This means for every dollar the company must pay to its vendors, creditors, etc. the company has two dollars of assets. Generally this is considered healthy as the company has more than enough current assets to pay off its current liabilities.

Example.
However, if a company has less current assets than current liabilities, there may be some liquidity issues. For example, the company only has $500 of current assets (cash, accounts receivable, inventory etc.) but it has $1,000 of current liabilities (accounts payable, income taxes payable, customer deposits, etc.), then the current ratio is 0.5:1. The company may not have enough liquid assets to pay off liabilities as they become due.

Even though some companies have a current ratio of less than 1, this may be normal for some industries or companies that are just starting up.

Example.
A company that is just starting up may not have generated enough cash to pay its liabilities. For some time it may need to rely on short-term or long-term financing from the bank or other creditor. This may be normal for start-ups, but over time, the current ratio should improve as the company stabilizes. If the current ratio does not improve or worse, deteriorate, then the company may be in financial trouble.

A current ratio of less than 1 may be normal for some industries. In that case, the benchmark should not be to see whether the current ratio is 1, but rather look at what the current ratio of other companies are in the industry. Compare to other companies is a good way to see if a company is performing better or worse than its competitors.

URL letter: ? (question mark)

9. Long-term assets - needed to generate future income

Now that we have looked at current assets and briefly discussed the current ratio, let us look at long-term assets.

Note:
When you look at financial statements, sometimes current assets are presented first followed by long-term assets, and other times long-term assets are presented first followed by current assets. Both are acceptable by *International Financial Reporting Standards.* Some parts of the world follow one presentation method, others follow the other.

Long-term assets includes:
- Property, plant and equipment
- Intangible assets
- Goodwill

Long-term assets are generally acquired in order to produce revenue in the future.

Let's look at some long-term assets in more detail in the next few sections.

URL letter: v

10. Property, plant and equipment (PP&E) - watch how they depreciate

This section of the balance sheet includes items like:
- Land
- Buildings
- Plants
- Equipment
- Vehicles
- Furniture
- Computers

Most businesses have items above, often called "fixed assets". PP&E are purchased for the purpose of producing income.

A company can buy land and build an office in order to meet with customers or clients to provide goods or services in order to make revenue. Equipment may be purchased to produce widgets. Vehicles can be purchased to deliver goods. Furniture and computers are used for services and administrative functions of the business with the goal of earning revenue.

Example.
When a company purchases PP&E, it must capitalize them onto the balance sheet as follows:

Dr. Computer   600
     Cr. Cash   600
To record purchase of capital asset

Then accounting rules require that the company depreciate the capital asset over its useful life.

Example.
The computer has a useful life of 3 years.

Dr. Depreciation - computer   200
     Cr. Accumulated amortization - computer   200
To record depreciation for the year

Because companies are allowed to make accounting estimates as to how long the useful life of an asset is, there may be incentive to depreciate more (thus lower income) or depreciate less (to give the impression of higher income).

It makes sense why a company has an incentive to give an impression of a higher income. Some reasons may be:

- Management bonuses are dependent on net income
- Bank covenants require a certain level of net income to prevent violation and bank calling of a loan

But sometimes management wants to *lower* income.

Example.
A company wants to pay less taxes. It chooses to depreciate a computer over 2 years instead of 3 years. Using the example above, this means each year the depreciation is $300 ($600 cost divided by 2 years) instead of $200 ($600 cost divided by 3 years). Thus net income is decreased by an additional $100.

You can see some information on the depreciation of capital assets in the notes to financial statements at the end of the financial statements. Usually the company will disclose the type of asset, the depreciation rate, and other pertinent information.

Having this information allows you to decide whether the company is choosing reasonable depreciation rates for its capital assets.

URL letter: = (equal sign)

11. Intangible assets - essential for some businesses

Intangible assets may include, but are not limited to:
- Customer lists
- Patents
- Trademarks
- Copyrights

For some companies, intangible assets are very important to its survival. A company that relies on a patent to produce only on product may not survive without the patent.

The above intangible assets may expire after a certain number of years. For example, the customer list may become outdated, and patents can expire.

It's prudent for the accountant/bookkeeper, business owner, or investor to dig deeper into the intangible assets account if this is a significant part of the company's business.

URL letter: r

12. Goodwill - test for impairment

Goodwill is generally generated when a company acquires another. It must be tested for impairment under accounting rules. Stakeholders should investigate whether the amount of goodwill is reasonable at least on an annual basis.

URL letter: see next chapter!

13. Total assets - read the notes and make sure they are all there

The sum of current assets and long-term assets is the total assets of a company. Note that sometimes there are assets that are not presented on the balance sheet. It would be prudent for a stakeholder to read through the notes to the financial statement thoroughly and understand the business model of the company before making financial decisions based on the financial statements.

Total assets is used in some profitability ratios such as *Return on Assets.*

URL letter: I (capital i)

14. Return on Assets - did the company make money?

An investor typically wants to know how much income he's making from the investment he's made in a company.

Example.
An investor invests in two companies in the same industry. In each company he invests $1,000. This is the company's total assets. The first company makes a net income of $200. The second company makes a net income of $400.

Remember:
Return on Assets = Net income / Average total assets

Usually the return on assets ratio is calculated using average total assets over 2 years as the denominator. For simplicity, We'll just use one year's total assets.

Example.
For the first company, the return on assets is $200 / $1,000 = 20%
For the second company, the return on assets is $400 / $1,000 = 40%

Which company gave the investor the better bang for the buck?

With all other things equal, the second company gave a greater return for the investor's investment.

Let's look at another ratio that uses *Total Assets.*

URL letter: o

15. Asset turnover ratio - how much revenue did the company make?

The asset turnover ratio compares the company's sales or revenues to its total assets.

Remember:
Asset turnover ratio = sales or revenues / total assets
The higher the asset turnover ratio, the better a company is performing.

Example.
Two companies are in the same industry. The first company has sales of $4 million and a total assets of $1 million. The second company has sales of $6 million and a total assets of $1 million.

Which company performed better on the asset turnover ratio?

For the first company, the asset turnover ratio is $4 million / $1 million = 4.0
For the second company, the asset turnover ratio is $6 million / $1 million = 6.0

All other things equal, the second company is making better use of its $1 million assets by turning over revenue that Is 6 times its total assets.

URL letter: o

16. Current liabilities - pay or face consequences

We have touched on current liabilities in our discussion of the current ratio. Here's a recap. You can skip to the next section if the information is still fresh in your mind.

Current liabilities include:
- Accounts payable
- Income taxes payable
- Customer deposits

These are examples of liabilities that the company is obligated to pay within the next year. There can be legal and other consequences such as bad creditor relationship or bad vendor relationships for not paying these current liabilities on time.

The current ratio takes current assets and divides the total by current liabilities.

Remember:
Current ratio = current assets / current liabilities

URL letter: w

17. Accounts payable - keep your cash. Delaying payment is good

Accounts payable is sometimes called *Trade and other payables.*

Accounts payable includes:
- Purchases on credit, such as purchases of inventory
- Bills such as telephone bills that have been received but not yet paid

Sometimes bills that have been received but not yet paid are classified as *accrued liabilities.*

Depending on how the company classifies its accounts, sometimes on the balance sheet the presentation is: *Accounts payable and accrued liabilities.*

Regardless of how the company classifies its payables, accounts payable is generally payable within the next year.

Question:
Is a large accounts payable always a bad thing?

Answer:
Not necessarily. Cash is usually the lifeblood of a company. If the company is able to delay payment, even for 30 days, it may help its liquidity and cash flow. Smart money managers know that if they can collect money faster and delay payments, it helps improve company cash flow.

Think of it this way: given the choice of paying a bill now with cash or paying it 30 days later, which would you choose?

From a financial point of view, it may be smarter to delay paying of the bill, and keep the cash in your pocket now so you can spend it on something else to help the business grow.

On the other hand, a really large accounts payable could indicate problems paying bills. If there is lots of cash on the balance sheet but also a large accounts payable, it could mean the company isn't paying its bills on time and there could be some money management issues.

When a company doesn't pay its bills on time, it can incur interest and penalties.

Example.
When a company or individual doesn't pay its credit card bills on time, it incurs unnecessarily interest and penalties that could potentially hurt the business in the long run.

Conclusion:
The size of accounts payable should be in balance between delaying payment and paying bills on time.

URL letter: _ (underscore)

18. Income taxes payable - do this legally to avoid going to jail

This is the corporate taxes owing to the government. The amount of the income taxes can determine whether the company is efficient at avoiding taxes.

Remember:
There are two terms when it comes to a company trying to minimize its taxes:
- Tax avoidance - this is using legal means allowed by the tax authorities for a business to minimize its taxes
- Tax evasion - this is illegal. This is to use illegal means to not pay taxes.

The government provides many incentives for companies through its tax system. For example, it may provide small & medium sized businesses a lower tax rate for a certain amount of revenue dollars. A company can either use management bonuses or dividends to lower the amount of revenue to take maximum advantage of the small business tax rate in a legal manner.

Some businesses like Apple and Samsung have their own in-house legal and tax department and uses complicated tax shelters to reduce the company's taxes. However, the laws are constantly changing and sometimes these companies get into tax issues with the tax authorities.

URL letter: - (dash)

19. Customers' deposits / deferred revenue - not your money...yet!

Sometimes customers are required to make a deposit on their purchase or for services to be rendered in the future.

Since accounting follows the *matching principle,* which means to match the revenues with the expenses in the same year, customer deposits received but goods or services not rendered must be classified as a liability until the goods or services have been provided to the customer or rendered.

The matching principle essentially is as follows.

Example.
A community center provides an annual swimming pass to its members. A member purchases an annual swimming pass on October 1, and the community center's year-end is December 31. The community center can recognize 3 months of revenue (October, November, December) during this fiscal year, but must delay recognizing the other 9 months of revenue in the next year as a liability on the balance sheet called deferred revenue or customer's deposits.

URL letter: f

20. Debts - are they bad or good? It depends

Is debt bad?

It depends on what a company or individual does with the debt. They may have to pay interest and principle on the debt right now, but in the future it may help them to earn revenue. Taking on debt beyond one's means is sometimes a bad idea, but if it can lead to income-generating opportunities, then the risk-reward balance should be considered.

Most businesses take on business loans or line of credit when starting their businesses, and may continue to use these to finance business expansions or operations.

How well management team manages these debts become important. If the rewards are greater than the cost, then the debt may be good.

Example.
The revenue earned is more than the interest payments made to the bank. This may justify leveraging debt in the business.

URL letter: see next chapter!

21. Short-term loans - necessary at crucial times

Short-term loans are payable within one year, and thus are classified as a current liability. The loan may be from an individual, another business, a bank, or other creditor.

If a company takes a long-term loan, the current portion must be classified as a current liability. This means the amount due within one year is reclassified each year from the long-term loan into a current liability.

URL letter: 0 (zero)

22. Long-term liabilities - a way to fund the business

These are liabilities that a company is contractually obligated to pay beyond one year. As discussed in the short-term loans section, the current portion of long-term liabilities must be classified as a current liability. This affects the current ratio which reflects the liquidity of a company.

Remember:
Current ratio = current assets / current liabilities

URL letter: d

23. Debt-to-equity ratio - screw this up at your own risk

A very common financial ratio used by investors or creditors to determine whether to invest or loan money to a company is the debt-to-equity ratio.

Remember.
Debt-to-equity ratio = total debt / total shareholder's equity

Example.
Many bank covenants require the debt-to-equity ratio to stay within a certain ratio, such as no more than 2:1. If the company's debt-to-equity ratio increases to over 2:1, meaning over $2 of debt for every $1 of equity, the bank may choose to call the loan immediately.

This creates a very bad situation for the company, so they will try their best to stay on side with the bank covenants. The bank covenants are put in place because if a company takes on too much debt, it increases the risk that the bank will not be able to collect its loan.

URL letter: see next chapter!

24. Shareholder's equity - who owns the company?

This section of the balance sheet may include, but not limited to:
- Common shares
- Retained earnings
- Accumulated other comprehensive income

Common shares represent the ownership of the company.

Retained earnings represent how much value a company has generated in income in past years. Generally the higher the retained earnings means higher income generated in the past. If a company experiences a loss in a year, this decreases retained earnings when the books are closed at year-end.

Remember.
- Revenue is usually in a credit position
- Expenses are usually in a debit position
- Retained earnings is usually is in a credit position

During the year-end closing, the following adjusting journal entry is done:

Example.
If revenues was $3,000 and expenses was $2,500, there is net income of $500. This is closed into retained earnings of credit $500.

Dr. Revenue   3,000
         Cr. Expenses   2,500
         Cr. Retained earnings   500
To close net income into retained earnings for year-end

On the other hand, if expenses exceed revenue, then retained earnings is decreased.

Example.
If revenues was $2,500 and expenses was $3,000, there is net *loss* of $500. This is closed into retained earnings of *debit* $500.

Dr. Revenue   2,500

            Cr. Expenses   3,000
Dr. Retained earnings   500
To close net income into retained earnings for year-end

In this case, since expenses exceed revenue, retained earnings is in a debit position of $500. Therefore, retained earnings is *decreased* by $500.

URL letter: Q

25. Return on equity - getting your investment money's worth

Another way to measure how well a company is doing is the return on equity (ROE) ratio.

Remember:
Return on equity = net income / shareholder's equity

Generally, the greater your income using a smaller equity portion means a better use of the available resources.

Investors often look at return on equity to determine whether an investment is worth their while.

URL letter: link is complete! Put all the letters after https://www.youtube.com to see video.

26. Income statement

The income statement is related to the balance sheet. As we discussed in the retained earnings section, at the fiscal year-end, the revenue and expenses gets closed into retained earnings on the balance sheet.

A big difference between the income statement and the balance sheet is that the income statement represents an accumulating total rather than a point in time.

Example.
A company's year-end is December 31. Its revenue from January 1 to December 31 is $500,000. The revenue on the income statement will state $500,000. This is the accumulated revenue for the full 365 days, not just one point in time. The income statement header will say something like:

Income Statement
For the year ended December 31

This is different from the balance sheet, which will say something like this:

Balance Sheet
As at December 31

Remember:
- The balance sheet is a snapshot at a particular time
- The income statement amounts are accumulated amounts over a period of time

27. Revenue - first thing most people look at

Most readers of financial statements look at this line first before anything else. Yes, revenue is so important to the livelihood of a company. In most cases, without revenue a company cannot survive very long.

As discussed earlier in the accounts receivable section, a company with a lot of recorded revenue or sales may not necessarily be in good financial shape. It could be recording a lot of sales, but if customers are not paying, revenues do not mean much. Eventually the company will run out of cash and declare bankruptcy or other drastic measures.

Remember:
It is important to look at a line on the financial statement such as revenue in conjunction with other accounts elsewhere in the financial statements. Revenue and accounts receivable is one such combination.

Another thing to note is that companies that experience explosive growth year after year may not necessarily succeed in the long run.

Some companies fuel their explosive growth through acquiring other companies and not through organic growth. In many cases, this is not a sustainable business model because of incompatibilities between the employees of the various companies acquired and the parent company, inconsistencies between IT systems, accounting systems, etc.

28. Cost of sales - let's keep this low

If the company is a manufacturing company, this will typically be the line underneath revenue. If the company is a services company, there is usually no cost of sales line on the income statement.

Cost of sales is related to the cost of inventory purchased. Cost of sales is subtracted from revenue to get gross margin, also known as gross profit.

Cost of sales and inventory are usually interrelated. If one goes up, the other should go up at a relatively similar increase. If one increases significantly and the other doesn't, this may warrant further investigation.

29. Gross margin / gross profit - did we make a profit?

This is usually a measurement of how well a company is doing with pricing its merchandise against what they paid to acquire the inventory or raw materials.

Gross margin shows whether a company is doing well against its competitor.

Gross margin is usually looked at in terms of revenue, a calculation known as gross profit margin.

Remember:
Gross profit margin = gross profit / revenue

Example.
A company can sell its widget for $15, and the cost to make the widget is $5. What is the gross profit margin?

The gross profit would be revenue $15 minus cost of goods sold $5 which equals $10.

Gross profit margin = $10 / $15 = 67%

This gross profit margin can be compared to that of competitors to see how well a company is doing with its pricing, which usually shows if it has a competitive advantage in its products.

Similar accounting margins include:
- Operating margin
- Net margin

Remember:
Operating margin = operating profit / sales
Net margin = net income / sales

30. Cash flows - cash is king

If a company's cash position has increased significantly from the previous year, it's prudent to see where that source of cash is from.

If the cash increase is from operations revenues, collection of accounts receivable, it's a good sign. You can see this in the statement of cash flows in the line called *cash flow from operations.*

However, if you look at the statement of cash flows and see most of the cash is from *cash flow from financing activities*, you'll want to be a little cautious. It means the money is coming from loans or investors are forking out more money from their own pockets.

If cash flow is from operations, it means the company is self-sustaining through the sale of its goods or services. If the majority of cash flow is from financing or investing activities, there can be some concern. It may be alright to have cash flow from financing or investing activities for a short period of time, to get enough funding so that operations can become more self-sustaining, but if year after year cash flow is coming from financing or investing activities, it can indicate that the business itself is not doing well.

Cash flow from investing activities could mean selling of capital assets.

Final thoughts

I hope you've found this book useful and can keep it at your desk as a quick reference tool.

IMPORTANT! Please go to Amazon's website and rate my book. It takes a minute to rate the number of stars and it will help other readers see that you enjoyed my book and so they can also benefit from it. Please also leave a comment on what you enjoyed most from the book. Leaving a comment is optional, but will be really helpful for my books to attract more readers so more people can benefit. I appreciate your assistance!

Click here to go to my Amazon Author page: http://goo.gl/4UQfJW. You can also search Amazon for "Calvin K Lee" for my other books. You will find them inspirational and improve the quality of your life.

Bonus video on balance sheet concepts

There are letters at the end of each chapter in this book. Add them to the end of this link to complete the URL:

https://www.youtube.com/

Click here to return

Praise for *"Bookkeeping and Accounting Step-by-step Basics for Small & Medium Sized Businesses and Home Businesses"*

"This is awesome! I love the short chapters with clear examples."

"I'm 100% certain to say that this book should be accounting 100 pre-requisite course for anyone who wants to take introduction to accounting! Very clear, concise, and concrete. Well done!"

 - K.T., CPA, CA

Praise from readers of Calvin's books:

"Very practical, good reading!"

"I really enjoy your books."

"Well done, very informative. I like how you used your example."

"By using his own example, Calvin gives hope for the readers."

"Great real life experience that you can relate to easily."

"Very clear, concise, and concrete. Well done."

"Practical tips and relatable examples. A pleasant read. Congratulations on your recent publications! Keep writing more."

"I've taken notes on my smart phone and will implement them in my life."

"Thanks for the little pearls of wisdom and optimism."

About the Author

Calvin K. Lee, MBA, CPA, CA, CPA (Illinois) is an accountant, author, composer, and teacher. He has lived in Beijing, Hong Kong, Toronto, and Vancouver, and travelled to many countries including the U.S.; to Europe such as the U.K., France, Italy, Germany, and Switzerland; and to Asia such as China, Malaysia, Singapore, Japan, and Thailand. Some of his favorite topics include love, relationships, effective communication, psychology, leadership, teamwork, and business. His biggest passion is inspiring and helping others achieve their goals. To do this, Calvin has been writing articles for his blog for over 10 years to inspire and encourage others.

Calvin holds an undergraduate degree from the University of British Columbia in Vancouver, a MBA degree with distinction from York University in Toronto, Canada and is expecting a Double MBA degree from Peking University in Beijing, China in 2016. He is a CPA designated accountant In the U.S. and Canada, and also a Chartered Accountant in Canada. In addition to his successful career in accounting, he has also taught Master of Accounting classes at university, taught accounting modules at the CPA professional association, and enjoys being a mentor to younger accountants. He has served as President of the MBA Ambassadors during his MBA studies and as Chair of the Young Professionals Forum at the CPA Association.

Note to the reader

This book is written for general guidance, and is not a substitute for accounting, legal, tax, or other professional advice with a qualified advisor. Laws are always changing. While every effort is made to make this book current, there may be errors or omissions. This book is made available with no representations or warranties of any kind for the accuracy or completeness of this book. The author and/or publisher do not assume and hereby disclaim any liability or responsibility for any action or decision leading to claims, losses or damages by any person(s) relying on the contents of this book. Consult a professional advisor as needed as the examples may or may not be applicable to your situation. The accounting standards discussed here follows standards pertaining to small & medium sized enterprises. While these bookkeeping & accounting concepts can be similar in other parts of the world, there may be some differences.

Contact the author

I welcome feedback and comments.

My e-mail address is hellocalvinlee@gmail.com.

Follow me on Twitter @calvinklee2010

If there are any topics you want me to write about in a future book, I'd love to know!

Other books by Calvin K. Lee

Click here to go to my Amazon author page with all my books. **Or click each link below for each book.**

1. How to Increase Confidence and Succeed in Meeting People: Business Networking the Easy Way: Meet New People Now! (Book #1)

2. Living an Extraordinary and Amazingly Purposeful Life: 9 Principles to a Better Life (Book #2)

3. Words of Wisdom, Encouragement, and Inspiration: Bring Happiness into Your Life (Book #3)

4. How to Work Smarter, Not Harder: Success in the Workplace (Book #4)

5. A Collection of Short Stories: And the Moral of the Story is...? (Book #5)

6. Bookkeeping and Accounting Step-by-step Basics for Small & Medium Sized Businesses and Home Businesses: Over 20 Examples of Common Accounting Transactions! (Book #6)

FREE book sample from

"How to Increase Confidence and Succeed in
Meeting People: Business Networking the Easy
Way...Meet New People Now!"

©2015 Calvin Lee
All rights reserved

How to Increase Confidence and Succeed in Meeting People: Business Networking the Easy Way

Meet New People Now!

CALVIN K. LEE, MBA

Table of contents

1. Defining networking
2. Can introverts become good at networking?
3. The benefits of networking
4. Networking like a pro
5. You never know who knows who!
6. Maintaining your network
7. Conclusion
8. About the author

Note to the reader

This book is written for general guidance, and is not a substitute for accounting, legal, tax, or other professional advice with a qualified advisor. Laws are always changing. While every effort is made to make this book current, there may be errors or omissions. This book is made available with no representations or warranties of any kind for the accuracy or completeness of this book. The author and/or publisher do not assume and hereby disclaim any liability or responsibility for any action or decision leading to claims, losses or damages by any person(s) relying on the contents of this book. Consult a professional advisor as needed as the examples may or may not be applicable to your situation.

CHAPTER 4: Networking like a pro

When I attend an event, I aim to start my networking at the top. Every event has limited time, and you have limited energy. You want the best bang for your buck. What I mean by starting at the top is to meet the organizers of an event. They will likely be wandering around the room with an officially looking nametag that is computer printed with a nice company logo, while the other participants are all wearing sticker nametags. Easy to spot!

Why should you start with the organizers of an event? They can easily introduce you to other people. They will likely know a lot of people in the room, and they can introduce you to other members of the organizing committee. In other words, they are a great resource to start. You should start there.

It's also easy to start a conversation with the organizers. You already know a lot about them. They organized the event. You can tell them they organized a great event, ask them how long it took to organize, how many guests are expected to come, etc. They will be glad to know you.

Don't worry so much about your own performance. If you focus and enjoy what the other person is saying, it takes a lot of pressure of you. People love to talk about themselves. Once you learn how to get people to talk about themselves, just open both ears and listen! Try it!

Click here now to get your copy from Amazon: *1. How to Increase Confidence and Succeed in Meeting People: Business Networking the Easy Way: Meet New People Now! (Book #1)*

FREE book sample from

"Living an Extraordinary and Amazingly Purposeful Life: 9 Principles to a Better Life"

©2015 Calvin Lee
All rights reserved

Living an Extraordinary and Amazingly Purposeful Life

9 Principles to a Better Life

Calvin K. Lee, MBA, CPA

Table of Contents

Table of Contents

1. What you'll get out of this book

2. Balance Sheet - things to watch for

3. Parts of the balance sheet

4. Is lots of cash always a good thing? Not always.

5. Accounts receivable and sales are going up. Great? Maybe not.

6. Inventory - beware of obsolescence

7. Current assets - your first line of defense in business liquidity

8. Current ratio: can this company survive 1 year?

9. Long-term assets - needed to generate future income

10. Property, plant and equipment (PP&E) - watch how they depreciate

11. Intangible assets - essential for some businesses

12. Goodwill - test for impairment

13. Total assets - read the notes and make sure they are all there

14. Return on Assets - did the company make money?

15. Asset turnover ratio - how much revenue did the company make?

16. Current liabilities - pay or face consequences

17. Accounts payable - keep your cash. Delaying payment is good

18. Income taxes payable - do this legally to avoid going to jail

19. Customers' deposits / deferred revenue - not your money...yet!

20. Debts - are they bad or good? It depends

21. Short-term loans - necessary at crucial times

22. Long-term liabilities - a way to fund the business

23. Debt-to-equity ratio - screw this up at your own risk

24. Shareholder's equity - who owns the company?

25. Return on equity - getting your investment money's worth

26. Income statement

27. Revenue - first thing most people look at

28. Cost of sales - let's keep this low

29. Gross margin / gross profit - did we make a profit?

30. Cash flows - cash is king

Final thoughts

Bonus video on balance sheet concepts

About the Author

Note to the reader

Contact the author

Other books by Calvin K. Lee

FREE book sample from

"How to Increase Confidence and Succeed in Meeting People: Business Networking the Easy Way...Meet New People Now!"

FREE book sample from

"Living an Extraordinary and Amazingly Purposeful Life: 9 Principles to a Better Life"

FREE book sample from

Words of Wisdom, Encouragement, and Inspiration

Calvin K. Lee, MBA, CPA

WORDS OF WISDOM, ENCOURAGEMENT, AND INSPIRATION (BOOK #3)

Bring Happiness into Your Life

FREE book sample from

How to Work Smarter, Not Harder: Success in the Workplace

FREE book sample from

A Collection of Short Stories

FREE book sample from

Bookkeeping and Accounting Step-by-step Basics for Small & Medium sized Businesses and Home Businesses: Over 20 Examples of Common Accounting Transactions!

Introduction

1. How do I step out of my comfort zone?

2. What are you thinking?

3. Be yourself

4. Know yourself

5. Don't let other people run your life

6. Set a S.M.A.R.T. goal!

7. Take risks!

8. Who do you want as friends?

9. Continuous learning

Final thoughts

About the author

Other books by Calvin Lee

Note to the reader

This book is written for general guidance, and is not a substitute for accounting, legal, tax, or other professional advice with a qualified advisor. Laws are always changing. While every effort is made to make this book current, there may be errors or omissions. This book is made available with no representations or warranties of any kind for the accuracy or completeness of this book. The author and/or publisher do not assume and hereby disclaim any liability or responsibility for any action or decision leading to claims, losses or damages by any person(s) relying on the contents of this book. Consult a professional advisor as needed as the examples may or may not be applicable to your situation.

Praise from readers for Calvin's books:

"Very practical, good reading!"

"I really enjoy your books."

"Well done, very informative. I like how you used your example."

"By using his own example, Calvin gives hope for the readers."

"Great real life experience that you can relate to easily."

"Very clear, concise, and concrete. Well done."

"Practical tips and relatable examples. A pleasant read. Congratulations on your recent publications! Keep writing more."

"Thanks for the little pearls of wisdom and optimism."

Introduction

Most people want to live an extraordinary life, but not everybody who wants to does.

With effort, I believe everyone and everybody who wants to live an extraordinary life can. In my own life, I've lived in four different cities, met hundreds of people from all over the world, and enjoy a career that I love. I consider my life extraordinary even though I am just a very normal, average person growing up in a normal, average household. The key is the attitude of the mind, as well as taking appropriate action.

Turn the page and let the journey begin!

1. How do I step out of my comfort zone?

People love their comfort zone. That's why they don't live extraordinary lives.

First of all, you have to have a deep desire for a better life, and you'll do anything to get it. And that means some temporary discomfort. People get bored of routine. You work the same job every day, but you don't change. The most likely reason is the current job is comfortable.

What I've found in my own journey is the decision to step out is the most difficult part. I remember going to zip line some years ago, where there is a wire hanging between two high poles with the rider strapped into a harness and fly across the two poles at a very fast speed.

We were required to climb up a really tall pole, the height of an electric cable pole, two or three stories high. As someone who is afraid of heights, climbing up the pole was scary, I had to remind myself to not look down. But climbing wasn't the scariest part. I remember there was a small platform at the top to sit on, the moment before you jump. I was horrified, petrified, mortified. I remember thinking to myself, "What did I get myself into?" After a few seconds of hesitation, which felt like eternity, I leaped off the platform, and had the thrill of my life zip lining. Once I made the jump, I was no longer afraid.

KEY POINT: To live an extraordinary and amazing life...You have to jump and take a leap of faith!

What does this mean in real life?

Several years ago I remember joining a volunteer committee for my profession to organize educational & social events for young professionals. I was a committee member and one day, the chairperson announced she was stepping down, and asked for volunteers to take over her role. I was excited at the opportunity, but I also had my doubts. Fear and worries flooded my mind:

Who am I to take this role? Do I have what it takes?

I don't have the experience.

What if I don't do a good job?

Knowing that the longer I hesitate the more worries and excuses my mind will come up with, I decided to take a leap of faith and just raise my hand and volunteer. The rest is history.

PUT IT INTO PRACTICE: Try to step out of your comfort zone a little everyday. That way, when a big decision comes up, you'll be more ready to take the leap of faith.

Do this, and you're well on your way to an extraordinary life!

Click here now to get your copy: *2. Living an Extraordinary and Amazingly Purposeful Life: 9 Principles to a Better Life (Book #2)*

FREE book sample from

Words of Wisdom, Encouragement, and Inspiration
©2015 Calvin Lee
All rights reserved

Calvin K. Lee, MBA, CPA

WORDS OF WISDOM, ENCOURAGEMENT, AND INSPIRATION (BOOK #3)

Bring Happiness into Your Life

Table of Contents

Introduction

1. How to be successful

2. Be thankful

3. Words of encouragement in pain and suffering

4. A brighter day will surely come

5. Words of wisdom on love

6. You are unique!

7. Fake it till you make it!

8. More words of wisdom

Final thoughts

About the Author

Other books by Calvin K. Lee

Note to the reader

This book is written for general guidance, and is not a substitute for accounting, legal, tax, or other professional advice with a qualified advisor. Laws are always changing. While every effort is made to make this book current, there may be errors or omissions. This book is made available with no representations or warranties of any kind for the accuracy or completeness of this book. The author and/or publisher do not assume and hereby disclaim any liability or responsibility for any action or decision leading to claims, losses or damages by any person(s) relying on the contents of this book. Consult a professional advisor as needed as the examples may or may not be applicable to your situation.

Praise from readers for Calvin's books:

"Very practical, good reading!"

"I really enjoy your books."

"Well done, very informative. I like how you used your example."

"By using his own example, Calvin gives hope for the readers."

"Great real life experience that you can relate to easily."

"Very clear, concise, and concrete. Well done."

"Practical tips and relatable examples. A pleasant read. Congratulations on your recent publications! Keep writing more."

"Thanks for the little pearls of wisdom and optimism."

1. How to be successful

Thomas Edison took more than 1,000 attempts to invent the electric light bulb. Did he say he failed 1,000 times? No, he said he was successful in finding 1,000 ways *not* to make a light bulb.

With every rejection, you are one step closer to success.

You reap what you sow. What you don't sow is what you won't reap.

There is a fire of passion inside of you. All you have to do is find it and rekindle it.

All successful people have a clear purpose and goal.

Thinking is hard work, which is why so few people do it. Those who can think succeed.

Everyone has the potential to succeed. Frequently it's not a lack of skill that prevents people from success, but rather fear: fear of the unknown, fear of rejection, fear of success, fear of rejection, fear of being different. What do you fear?

It is said the journey of a thousand miles begins with a single step. Success does not come overnight, it comes through a series of steps. Sometimes it's two steps forward and one step back.

Don't despair. Every setback and rejection brings you one step closer to your goal.

You know you can do it. Believe in yourself!

If it is to be, why not me?

Successful people are always looking for opportunities to help others. Unsuccessful people are always asking, "What's in it for me?"

If you've never failed, it means you've never tried. If you've never tried things beyond your comfort zone, you've likely never failed.

Money spent can be re-earned, but experience is mine to keep for the rest of my life.

If you want to succeed, cut the following from your vocabulary: "I should have", "I could have", "I would have". Now take concrete action.

The difference between winners and ordinary people is winners follow through despite fear while others just dream and take no action.

Learning to delay instant gratification is crucial to success. A research study put a child in an empty room with a cookie in front of them. The researcher tells the child he will leave the room for a while. The child can choose to take the cookie, but if the child can wait until the researcher comes back, the researcher will give the child two cookies. The research showed children that can wait and delay instant gratification are more successful in life.

Click here now to get your copy on Amazon: *3. Words of Wisdom, Encouragement, and Inspiration: Bring Happiness into Your Life (Book #3)*

FREE book sample from

How to Work Smarter, Not Harder: Success in the Workplace

©2015 Calvin Lee
All rights reserved

HOW TO WORK SMARTER, NOT HARDER (BOOK #4)

CALVIN K. LEE, MBA, CPA

Success in the Workplace

Table of Contents

About the Author

Introduction: smart ways to work

1. Techniques to instantly brighten up your day: smile and whistle

2. Working smarter: know if you're a morning person or a night owl

3. Change your attitude and approach

4. Exercise becomes more important as busyness increases

5. Improve your biggest asset: your mind

6. Meditation: it gives you a sense of more time

7. Improve your creativity by doing something relaxing

8. Know yourself: your personality, likes & dislikes, strengths & weaknesses

9. Avoid multitasking: finish one task before starting another

10. Improve attention span

Final Thoughts

Other Books by Calvin K. Lee

Note to the reader

This book is written for general guidance, and is not a substitute for accounting, legal, tax, or other professional advice with a qualified advisor. Laws are always changing. While every effort is made to make this book current, there may be errors or omissions. This book is made available with no representations or warranties of any kind for the accuracy or completeness of this book. The author and/or publisher do not assume and hereby disclaim any liability or responsibility for any action or decision leading to claims, losses or damages by any person(s) relying on the contents of this book. Consult a professional advisor as needed as the examples may or may not be applicable to your situation.

Introduction: smart ways to work

There are many ways to work, but some ways are smarter than other ways. For example, how many ways there are to get from San Francisco to New York City? Here are some options:

1. Walk there
2. Run there
3. Ride a bicycle there
4. Drive a car there
5. Take a plane there

All of these ways will get you from San Francisco to New York City...eventually. It's just that some ways are smarter than other ways. All of these ways eventually work, but some ways are smarter and more efficient than others. In today's day and age, time is of the essence. You've heard the saying, "Time is money."

KEY POINT: there are multiple ways to solve every problem, but some ways are smarter than other ways.

Some of the suggestions in this book can be implemented immediately and effortlessly, immediately improving your work life. Other suggestions take time to change an old habit to a new one. Be patient with yourself while trying to change. It takes effort but you will receive huge dividends later.

Kids are incredibly creative. If you ask them to stand in the corner and face the wall, they will find a fun way to spend the time there. They will invent a game with himself or herself, sing a song, wave their arms, or see how long they can hold their breath.

I love watching kids play at the park. They are incredibly creative in what they do. They don't need people to tell them how to play. They innately know how to have fun. Unfortunately, as we grow to be adults we lose that sense of creativity. We think there is one "right" way to do things, and we do it over and over again. Fortunately for us, we all have a kid living inside of us. We were once kids, with limitless imagination and energy. But our school system taught us to sit still, learn the 'right' way to do things, and just follow what others do.

KEY POINT: Each of us can let the creative child inside of us be imaginative and have fun. In the creative process, you'll find smarter ways to work!

We can tap into our imagination and find smarter ways to do things. Let the creative child inside of you blossom again. You'll experience life in a whole new way doing your routine tasks!

PUT IT INTO ACTION: For every task you do, try to find a smarter way to do it. Be creative and have some fun!

1. Techniques to instantly brighten up your day: smile and whistle

If you're in a happy mood, you work smarter than when you are in a grumpy mood. There are many simple ways to lift your mood and brighten up your day within minutes.

KEY POINT: You work smarter when you're in a good mood.

The first way is to smile, whether you feel like it or not. Once I was really stressed out at work. I had nothing to smile about, but I forced my face to smile. Doing that changes the chemistry in your body that actually makes you feel better. It's true when you feel a certain emotion, your body would physically mimic that emotion. For example, if you feel happy, your face would naturally smile. The reverse is also true. If you make your body physically do something, you will start feeling the accompanying emotion.

Another way to instantly brighten up your day is to whistle, or hum a song. It's hard to whistle and feel grumpy at the same time. You've probably heard the song lyrics that go, "whistle while you work." It will make you happier instantly. Then you can work smarter.

PUT IT INTO ACTION: smile even if you don't feel like it. Whistle if your work place allows it, or hum quietly to yourself. All of these simple yet powerful techniques can lift your mood within a short period of time and significantly improve the quality of your work. You can also try other actions like snapping your fingers or clapping your hands.

Click here now to get your copy from Amazon: *4. How to Work Smarter, Not Harder: Success in the Workplace (Book #4)*

FREE book sample from

A Collection of Short Stories
©2015 Calvin Lee
All rights reserved

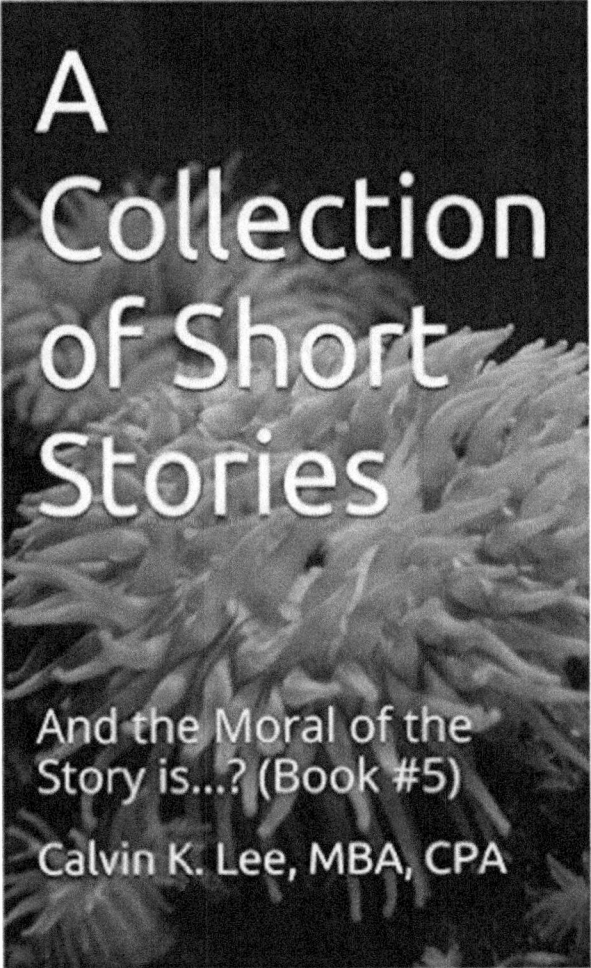

A Collection of Short Stories

And the Moral of the Story is...? (Book #5)

Calvin K. Lee, MBA, CPA

Table of Contents

About the Author

To the reader

The flag and pole (adapted from the blockbuster movie *Captain America*)

The red and blue crayons

The train

Five planks of wood: unity is power

The magical watches

A school of fish

The well

The animal trap and a benevolent man

Contact the author and final words

Other books by Calvin K. Lee

The flag and pole (adapted from the blockbuster movie *Captain America*)

You can find a video clip of this on Youtube by searching "Captain America pole scene".

A drill sergeant told his unit of soldiers that they were going to have a test. The test will test their physical strength and decision-making ability.

First, the sergeant made the soldiers do pushups. Then they had to crawl through mud. After that they had to run miles throughout the training fields.

Finally, they arrived at their final test. The drill sergeant stood next to tall pole and shouted, "Listen up, soldiers! There's a flag attached to the top of this pole. The first person to get it and bring me the flag passes the test. The rest will have to do pushups, crawl through the mud, and run miles again."

The men jumped on the pole one by one and tried to climb up the pole to get the flag. However, the sergeant in advance had coated the pole with oil so it was really slippery and the soldiers couldn't get a solid grip to climb. They kept sliding back down, often landing on top of each other. "Nobody's gotten that flag in 17 years!" shouted the drill sergeant. After many failed attempts, the soldiers were exhausted and was considering giving up, that the task was impossible.

At this time one of the soldiers, Rogers, walked up to the pole and said he will get the flag. The other soldiers, who were bigger and stronger than Rogers, laughed. They called him "Skinny Rogers" because of his lack of physical strength and skinny frame.

Rogers walked up to the pole, and calmly pulled out the metal piece out of the ground that held the pole vertical. The pole fell to the ground with a thud like a tree being cut down, leaving the flag that was on top of the pole on the ground.

"Hey, that's cheating!" said the other soldiers.

Rogers calmly said, "The sergeant just told to get the flag and bring it to him. He never said taking the pole down was against the rules." Rogers then looked at the sergeant.

"He is correct!" said the sergeant with a smile. "This is not only a test of physical strength, but a test of your decision-making skills and ability to carefully pay attention to instructions! Now all of you, with the exception of Rogers, do your push ups, crawl through the mud, and run miles again!"

Click here to get your copy from Amazon: _5. A Collection of Short Stories: And the Moral of the Story is...? (Book #5)_

FREE book sample from

Bookkeeping and Accounting Step-by-step Basics for Small & Medium sized Businesses and Home Businesses: Over 20 Examples of Common Accounting Transactions!

BOOKKEEPING AND ACCOUNTING STEP-BY-STEP BASICS FOR SMALL & MEDIUM SIZED BUSINESSES AND HOME BUSINESSES

CALVIN K. LEE, MBA, CPA

Over 20 examples of common accounting transactions! (Book #6)

Praise for *"Bookkeeping and Accounting Step-by-step Basics for Small & Medium Sized Businesses and Home Businesses"*

"This is awesome! I love the short chapters with clear examples."

"I'm 100% certain to say that this book should be accounting 100 prerequisite course for anyone who wants to take introduction to accounting! Very clear, concise, and concrete. Well done!"

- K.T., CPA, CA

Praise from readers of Calvin's books:

"Very practical, good reading!"

"I really enjoy your books."

"Well done, very informative. I like how you used your example."

"By using his own example, Calvin gives hope for the readers."

"Great real life experience that you can relate to easily."

"Very clear, concise, and concrete. Well done."

"Practical tips and relatable examples. A pleasant read. Congratulations on your recent publications! Keep writing more."

"I've taken notes on my smart phone and will implement them in my life."

"Thanks for the little pearls of wisdom and optimism."

Table of Contents

Introduction
Your first day on the job as a bookkeeper or accountant

Types of accounts in accounting

Balance sheet and income statement

Debits and credits must equal

Assets

Liabilities

Revenue

Expenses

Taxes

Accounts receivable

Accounts payable

Purchasing inventory

Inventory costing methods

Lower of cost or market (LCM)

Capital assets

Depreciation of capital assets

Sale of an asset

Shareholder loans – shareholder pays out of pocket

Shareholder loans – company pays on behalf of shareholder

Year-end closing

About the author

Note to the reader

Contact the author

Other books by Calvin K. Lee

Introduction

After reading this book, you will be able to do basic bookkeeping with confidence.

Accounting is the language of business. Whether the company is a global Fortune 500 company or a local mom and pop shop, both of these companies need a system to keep track of income, expenses, assets purchased like computers or furniture, liabilities obtained like mortgages, and equity components such as number of shares issued or how much the owner has invested in the company. Of course, the bigger the company and the more transactions it has, the more complex the accounting.

Small & medium sized businesses and home businesses do not need sophisticated accounting software. They just need a simple system to keep track of the company's transactions. This book is written for beginners to accounting and bookkeeping.

I am a designated CPA accountant in both Canada and the U.S., and have worked since 2007 as an accountant and auditor in public accounting firms and companies. The majority of my clients were small to medium sized businesses. Some of my clients' bookkeepers struggle with the accounting software and the basic accounting concepts.

I have also taught accounting courses at York University's reputable Schulich School of Business in Toronto while I was obtaining a MBA degree myself there. I taught in the Bachelor of Business Administration (BBA) program and Master of Accounting (MAcc) program.

I enjoyed teaching accounting concepts to first year students, and I understand that many of them struggle to learn the accounting language. Textbooks are sometimes long and difficult to follow. My greatest satisfaction in teaching is to explain a concept that is challenging a student, and watch a proverbial light bulb light up as they begin to understand the concept.

Since you've picked up this book, I believe you want to learn the basic concepts of accounting and bookkeeping for small & medium sized enterprises and home businesses. *I will use the simplest language to explain basic concepts so that you can perform accounting and bookkeeping duties for your business or company.*

This book is designed to be as practical as possible, so I'm going to focus on application rather than explaining detailed theory and concepts.

Think of this book as a quick reference guide rather than a detailed textbook. Therefore, it does not cover all the topics in a first year accounting course. This book covers the most common transactions an entry accountant or bookkeeper will do on a daily basis.

Click here now to get your copy from Amazon: *6. Bookkeeping and Accounting Step-by-step Basics for Small & Medium Sized Businesses and Home Businesses: Over 20 Examples of Common Accounting Transactions! (Book #6)*